THE
BOOK OF
COMMON
BETRAYALS

THE
BOOK OF
COMMON
BETRAYALS

LYNNE
KNIGHT

Winner of the
DOROTHY BRUNSMAN
POETRY PRIZE
2002

THE BOOK OF COMMON BETRAYALS
© 2002 by Lynne Knight
All Rights Reserved

Printed in the United States of America
by Ed's Printing in Chico, California

10 9 8 7 6 5 4 3 2 1

Bear Star Press
185 Hollow Oak Drive
Cohasset, CA 95973
www.bearstarpress.com

Cover: *Golden Round* by Jessica Colasanto
Author photograph: Kathleen Lynch
Book design: Beth Spencer

The publisher would like to thank Dorothy Brunsman,
as always, for her generous donation of the prize.

Library of Congress Control Number: 2002104744
ISBN: 0-9719607-0-4

ACKNOWLEDGMENTS

Thanks to the poets in Times Ten (www.timestenpoets.com) for their help with many of these poems and for their generosity of mind and spirit; to Kathleen Lynch, for staying alive for us all; to Melody Lacina, for her excellent proofreading; to my daughter, Jessica Colasanto, for the cover painting and so much more; and to the editors of the following journals, where some of these poems first appeared:

Beloit Poetry Journal: "Blue Thread: An Elegy"; "Boundless Kingdom";
    "The Map of Betrayal"; "The Model"; "Penitent"
Iowa Review: "The Unlimited Mood"
Kenyon Review: "For a Friend Whose Love Has Left"
North American Review: "None of Us at Prayer"
North Dakota Quarterly: "The Cordoning"; "The Dead Stop, They Just
    Stop"; "Talking About the Weather"
Ontario Review: "These Are the Conditions, Then"
Poetry: "Letter After the Diagnosis"; "Now There Were More of
    Them"
Poetry East: "I Don't Want All of You"
Poetry Northwest: "Archer"; "Bed and Bone"; "Bloodstreams";
    "Border Wars"; "Common Betrayals"
    "Meditation Interrupted by Bats"; "Night Food";
    "The Older Student's Story"; "Supper"; "Their Bodies Lay
    So Far"; "Winter Flowers"; "The Year Before the Breakup"
Poets On: "Rituals"
Southern Humanities Review: "If the Names of Things Could Be Relied
    On"; "In Itself Nothing"; "Lost Sestina"; "The Sphere
    of Cézanne's Apples"
Southern Review: "The Double"; "The Muse of the Actual"
Tar River Poetry: "Red Camellias Smashed by Week-Long Rain"

"I Don't Want All of You" is reprinted in *Who are the Rich, Where Do They Live?* (*Poetry East*, Numbers Forty-Nine and Fifty, 2000).

"Lost Sestina" was awarded the Theodore Christian Hoepfner Award for 1996 by *Southern Humanities Review*.

"The Muse of the Actual" is reprinted in *Best American Poetry 2000*.

"Song Beginning in Big Sleep" appears in *GRRRRR: An Anthology of Bear Poems* (Arctos Press, 2000).

TABLE OF CONTENTS

ONE: THE UNLIMITED MOOD

TWO: BED AND BONE

THREE: THE MAP OF BETRAYAL

for Michael

ONE

THE UNLIMITED MOOD

And like everyone, I took, I was taken
I dreamed

I was betrayed:

Earth was given to me in a dream
In a dream I possessed it

                    Louise Glück

LETTER AFTER THE DIAGNOSIS

This is the window I love best. It looks down
on roses, ferns, ivy the deer come to eat
once the rains have gone. Earlier I watched
a deer take a Peace rose in one nip. He held it

in his mouth, head dipping and lifting, the flutter
of petals like foam at his wide lips. Just when
I thought the sweet smell had made him drunk,
he swallowed. Then he nipped another. The same

intoxicated dance, head and forelegs lifting,
falling, in slow syncopation. After the fifth rose,
the bushtop stripped, I opened the window
to yell *Hey! Enough!* The deer looked up,

then strolled off through high grass. I tell you this
because I need some deer insouciance
to offer you against your fear. I did not
think of you at all while I watched the deer

eat the roses. But now I know if you had been
beside me, you would have put out your hand
to stop me from raising the window, you would have
done all you could to grant him abundance.

THE UNLIMITED MOOD
for Forrest Hamer

Sleepless late one night I examined the infinitive:
to place. What would be the agent?
Hands, memory: I tried to place him.
After a while, I remembered.
He was the one in love with bones.
In love with water over bones that had been thrown
from ships like scraps from meals,
like slops, like next to nothing
though he knew the record of that suffering
would make its way along the seafloor
to the coast, ooze up through heavy sand,
flood through reed and marsh grass,
spread through earth, disturb the foot of someone walking—
not stones but a calling, heaved against the insole—
until he lay his whole length down on sunwarmed grass,
pressing his good ear to cries and moans
blue at their center, blue in their nimbus,
blue as the water they had sunk through.
He would lie listening to these blues
and know to place their origin
in salty waters rising from the heart,
ancestral tears he would not know
what to do with until he thought to sing,
and, singing, heard the dead
instruct him where to place his grief: *Here.*
Where sorrows wash across your face
and disappear.

FOR A FRIEND WHOSE LOVE HAS LEFT

For a week now, the deer has been roaming
the neighbor's sloped and wooded yard,
dipping his antlers to leaf and blade.
The neighbor talks to him, and though parts
of the shrubs are vanishing, and the roses
will be gone if this keeps on,
the neighbor's voice is kind,
low, almost wooing.
Yesterday afternoon, the deer lay
in the grassy patch below the scrub oaks,
and the neighbor, talking low, moved
almost near enough to touch him.
This morning more deer came,
a doe and two fawns.
The neighbor, out for the morning paper,
greeted them all with such warmth
I half expected the deer to wave
their thin legs, or smile.
But they only moved their heads
with a slight sway of the proprietary,
waiting until he'd gone
to dip their heads and eat again.
They've come because the hills are dry.
They bring him calm, the neighbor says.
Here and there they've eaten branches bare,
but still, he hopes they'll stay until the rains.
Then another year will end.
Across the bay, you'll watch the hills give way
to green the deer will feed on
before drought drives them down again.
Bitterness, but of necessity.

LOST SESTINA

*Leonardo's portrait of Ginevra de' Benci was painted
c. 1478–80. Only one line of poetry written by Ginevra has
survived, the opening of a sestina, which reads: "I ask
your forgiveness and I am a mountain tiger."*

—Mary D. Garrard

I ask your forgiveness and I am a mountain tiger,
waiting. Deny me, and my fur bleeds white
while I roam stone peaks that seem from here
(you lift your head to gaze) not of this world—
ideas some hand contrived from tempera or oils.
Deny me, and my white paws turn all nail.

But you would not have me suffer, not drive the nail
of your withholding through my heart. *My tiger*,
you've called me, rubbing your face against the oils
you've rubbed into my breasts and thighs, so white
they seem like snow, if snow could burn. The world
was no more than our chamber. *Yes, here*—

but then our tongues took over, we could not hear
above the blood roar I could feel down to the nail
as I held myself above you, the known world
blurring as trees and shadows must when tigers
rush all tooth and sinew for the kill. O white
annihilation, and afterward the aromatic oils

glistening on us both, heat and sweat and oils
mixed. Sweet lord, is memory to be my enemy? *Here
is my heart*, you told me, and held out your hand: white
but for the short dark hairs and yellowing nails.
I asked your forgiveness. Then I waited: as a tiger
stands in the still of the forest I stood in the world

of our chamber thinking how little anyone's world
amounted to—small heap of bones. Leonardo's oils
would outlast us. How you raged I was his prey, tiger
that would fall into his arms if he desired! Here,
where I have played the soft wood to your nail,
indulged your wildest fancy, lain still and white

while you tongued me from my ankles to my eyes, white
with my ecstasy—raged that I'd betrayed you and your world.
Then that baleful glare—each eye sharpened like a nail
by your suspicions. . . . But my fur sinks thick, the oils
in my body warm me. I'll outwait, outwit you, here
or anywhere—make you rue the day you whispered *Tiger*,

wanting me wilder. No, these oils will crack before your tiger
comes to you white and panting as she once did. I'll wait here,
tending my nails while you hunt in other women, cold as oils.

THE MODEL

The model is dreaming of vegetables.
Tomatoes and rutabaga, butternut squash,
leeks, cabbages spill onto the table
at her side. Some of the students draw them.
Some draw her, trying to think of sex as natural
as vegetables, another set of gestures, an
attitude. They have been studying attitude.
Their instructor has told them art is attitude.
They know this does not mean what it otherwise
means: *She's got an attitude.* Though this model
definitely seems to have one. The way she never
covers herself during break, just sips at her Evian
and reads. The way she leans back so her breasts
won't sag, her stomach will flatten. They don't see her

as she sees herself, dressed in a cotton shift,
her hair pinned up, cooking a harvest feast
for her family. In this part of the dream,
the scene never changes: a stone house,
the sky bright with a cease-fire that's holding,
goats bleating on the stony hillside,
the figures around the table laughing and
talking, words strange to the ear as *rutabaga,
squash* . . . Then time gets confused. The sky
pulls apart, there are shells, body parts in the
street—legs, hands, teeth . . . or bones
splintered into teeth . . . Her long wooden spoon
dips into the pot . . . They will start with good wine,
toast the bright moon, Earth's bounty . . .

NIGHT FOOD

At the sweet spice house, we ate and ate,
my lost brother and I opened our mouths
and took in cornices and sills, latticework,

while at the back of our knees, shadows
from the forest rubbed like beasts, fur
of our terror pouring itself into the night

where the moon climbed, shrinking.
The house was the body of our mother.
The breasts were the spaces we fell into

when we had eaten so much the frame
began to sink into itself like a woman
who'd eaten the vowels from her keening.

My brother knew none of this.
Whenever he came to me, we set off
for the pathlessness, saying nothing

so our senses would not intervene.
Once at the house, we started on the side
still warm with sun. The sweetness then!

When we couldn't eat a bite more,
we would start back through the forest.
I can't tell all that happened then,

night fell so deep. But sometimes I held
still while we bled into each other
like shadows sinking as they spread.

NOW THERE WERE MORE OF THEM

They were fleeing through the forest
like the children in the story
only now there were more of them,
children, women, even men
too old or maimed to be of use.
The capable men already taken.
Nothing for those remaining but to flee
the takers, who would take her if she
slipped or lost her breath though she was
strong, at twenty, strong enough to make it.
The deeper they fled everything blurring
together like the shadows in her terrors or
words to the story her mother once read to her
over and over. The trees closer together
and in the green blind overhead,
birds singing. . . . She ran. She could hear
her breath like the child at the story:
Go on. Go on. Then images rushing from
the dark mesh of tree trunks:
Blood. Men's faces, grimacing
with lust. Legs forced open—women's, girls'.
In the green overhead, the birds never
stopped, their cries so loud and various
she could not tell her mother's cries. . . .
And now she did slip, her foot
catching in a dirt pocket, the tree
she stumbled against so calm, so still
she embraced it. Then bent to massage
her ankle. How easy to make the noose—
a child could do it, and the tree so adequate . . .

Pure chance, that the photographer found her body hanging
in the trackless forest. The shot taken
of her back, to spare us. And the next day

all of us staring at her picture in the paper
with the same terror we felt at the story
we were too young to read
though we had the rhythms by heart,
knew every word like our blood.

THE OLDER STUDENT'S STORY

In the war, he tended the wounded.
He saw bodies torn open like packages
from home. Sometimes he dreams
about it, but he's not one of the ones
who came home to wash his hands
over and over. It was never on his mind
like a woman he'd had and had to keep
having, just to prove something—no,
he wasn't wounded. But some of the
wounds he saw were bad, bad, worse
than the worst things in movies.
They could have won the war
if they'd gone all out, but instead
the government let them get blown
to bits like packages from home.
He keeps coming back to that
because one day, one of the last
on his tour, he tended a boy whose
wounds were crawling with ants,
like somebody left a box of sweets
out in the open. Before he could get
all the ants out, the boy died. He hardly
thinks about it now. If he decided
to write about O'Brien's "How
to Tell a True War Story"
for his essay, would it be okay
to include his own experience?
Or should he stick to the text?

THESE ARE THE CONDITIONS, THEN

If I'd locked the door that night—
If I'd slept less deeply—
If he'd chosen another floor
in the 20-story building—
If I'd lived in a different city—
If I'd understood the dream
the night before, with its
logs and wild horses,
its cold wind—
If I'd been stronger and had shoved
him from my body and then fled—
If violence were not a force
that rules like gravity—
If I'd screamed—
If his hands had not been wrapped
around my throat—
If he hadn't asked my name—

Or if I could tell you how still I lay
while he took my body,
how I can still hear the door closing
after him,
how still I lay
while my body
came back to me,
arm by thigh by throat by hand—
how I washed it and washed it,
numb as someone washing
the corpse of one she'd loved

COMMON BETRAYALS

The first one I don't remember.
Then I was walking down the road, new shoes,
heard the Blue Lady calling
and kept right on going. Her song
was too mournful, she never used words.
Or maybe I already knew she was nothing
but a common garden bird.

The next ones belong to everyone.
I swore I'd never touched the broken watch.
Never taunted kids from the bad end of town
for wearing the same clothes all week long.
Stole, yes, but was afterwards unable
to see the brightness of penny candy.

Then the nights I let one of them love me
while I cried out to another,
not a name, not even words,
just sound I would later hear
from the downstairs rooms. Fabrics
draining of color, floorboards
letting go of their nails

while the moon—because I watched,
it seemed—pulled a cloud
over its face, thick cloth
of the confessional.
Even then, my heart would not yield.
Everywhere, signs of treachery—
how this lobelia by my window

loosens its blue at dusk
to lighter blue, edged pink,
until it seems more cloud (displaced)

than flower. They say the faces
of the penitent glow whiter
than the lily at the moment of remorse,
though this too might be illusion.

MEDITATION INTERRUPTED BY BATS

No one knew how it happened, but one day
the soul disappeared like a rumor. Only the poet
was terrified enough to search for it. Standing
on the back porch every night while the stars
went on and the wind, the wind, what language
was this, just on the edge of coherence.
And inklike streaks overhead—bats, which were
not dark souls, as the ignorant once believed.
No, only think of that *Nature* special, the woman
whose pet bat, hanging asleep from her collar,
came to and crawled inside her blouse
as she looked into the camera saying
People spread all these rumors. . . .

But we were on the back porch in search
of the soul, rumored to be no more than rumor.
Should we go down the steps, walk under
the pines, murmuring as if at any moment
we might begin to speak in tongues and prove
the soul is real? —How cool the nights grow.
We should go back in for a sweater.
Maybe finish the letter we've been writing
for years, the one where we explain betrayal
as survival. For who among us is not guilty?
If the soul is real, it's probably small,
dark, batlike; and like the bat capable
of hanging for hours unobserved.

In the next part of the special on bats,
the basso voice told of bats that live
in dormant volcanoes. Then two bold men
descended with sturdy rope to observe
multitudes of bats, shrieking and swooping

and generating such terrible heat that no one
watching could not think of Hell. But Hell
might also be a rumor. In the letter we've been
writing, there is no way of naming the moment
of betrayal. It seemed more a sensation
than an act of will. Like fabric pulling apart.
Or skin. At the part of the back just beyond
reach. Where wings would start, if we had them.

IN ITSELF NOTHING

You're sitting in a room filled with edges.
If you took away that wall, this book, your chair,
the edges that were there would disappear.
In itself, the edge is nothing.
An imagined line between two objects.
If you tried to draw the edge of this book,
for example, you would draw the book, then

your hand or the table where the book has lain,
the shadings in between. But these lines
aren't edge: the book simply ends
or begins; the edge of your hand is no more
substantial than the edge of its shadow
on the table or the wall, itself an intervention
of the air, which has no edge,

like skin. This is what Rodin understood.
Not the embrace but its continuing as the body continues
in its longing to pass through
the border of the other:
marble to flesh, flesh to air,
pure mingling.
But that would take forever, and the lovers

are not myth. Their legs grow cold,
they begin to despise each other a little
for the truths they have told.
What they would give
to go back to the first sweetness,
their tongues small rivers
in the stone. But they are form. They lie

like great stone echoes of moments
when the skin becomes fire

that could burn through any border.
Listen to the sadness afterwards, they say.
All that heat gone as the edge is gone
when a wall subsides in ruin, a book falls
shut, the hand of the beloved is withdrawn.

SONG BEGINNING IN BIG SLEEP

The poet loves the bear who sleeps
such a long time in his skin. The bear
might stand like a man, eat like a man,

but it's the big sleep that makes the poet
fall in love with the bear's going still
while his world disappears under snow.

So each spring, when the river runs
and the bear shakes off the last of
sleep like drops of water caught in fur,

the poet dreams of winter. First the pines
stiffen in wind. Then crows start to streak
across the snow, the river runs colder,

the bear sleeps. If the poet could get close
without rousing the bear, she would hear
a sound like fur stirred by wind. But the bear

keeps hidden, sleeping to live. Or it will keep
hidden, when winter comes—it's still spring,
remember, and the poet's only dreaming

of winter, learning to let go of every desire
but finding the way from river to meadow,
past the last asters to the heaved granite.

The only thing she can take to the cave
is willingness to sleep. Will it be enough?
She lies still remembering that some bears

peel grapes with nothing but their teeth.
The poet thinks of the song this would make.
A close-up song, like blood on bone.

Thin, so thin the wind might never pick it up.

She will have to do it, then . . .

NONE OF US AT PRAYER

The first morning the dogwood flowered,
we slowed down to watch the petals guttering
above the ravine floor. The trees were candelabra,
this had been said many times before, the woods
a cathedral, that too, but we were young, innocent
of names already given. We knew picking dogwood
was forbidden, so we dreamed of sneaking out
while others slept to break whatever branches
we could reach and run with them like torches
through the tunnel of oak and maple that by day
was just the street we lived on. We would whirl
and spin the white-tipped branches until the flames
thinned, then wait while our senses calmed, the petals
reignited. The first one I touched shocked me with
its thickness, its wet. The pale bracts swirled pink
at their centers were the wounds of Christ, the nuns
had told us, and if we were pure in prayer, our palms
might open someday and bleed of their own accord
as the dogwood bled while we dreamed our way
through the tunnel, lit by our stolen torches.

Years passed and still none of us had dared to pick
one branch, even one blossom, for fear we would be
mutilating the persistent body of Christ, though by now
we were old enough to know the stigmata came from
hysteria, probably sexual hysteria, unholy fervor.
And we were old enough to sneer at descriptions
of dogwood as candelabra, at dreams of weaving
white torches through the night. If we sneaked out
for anything, it was boys, who waited like trees
in the dark and pulled us into them, wordlessly. So
whoever broke the first one off that morning
on the way to school, slid the jagged sprig
through the buttonhole of her blazer lapel, saying

So let them arrest me, none of us could say
with certainty now. Maybe none of it happened.
Maybe none of us lay dreaming of the flames
of dogwood dipping and arcing while we made
our strange circling procession. But we are all
marked by it. Look at my palms, the emptiness.
The cathedral in ruins, and none of us at prayer.

TWO

BED AND BONE

So we live here, forever taking leave.

Rainer Maria Rilke

BLUE THREAD: AN ELEGY

A discovery ship . . . had to go long distances in unfamiliar
waters and had to be able to sail into the wind . . . Its important
cargo was news, which could be carried in a small parcel, even in
the mind of one man . . .
                              —Daniel J. Boorstin, ***The Discoverers***

WOODEN SPOOL

Two girls playing at death.
One's mother died the month before,
and when she kneeled at the coffin,
she watched the strange skin for signs.
I'm going to make you a shroud, she says
to her friend. Pulls a blue sheet from her bed.
Stands holding it, looking out the window
where late summer leaves weave another
kind of shroud. Torn, like the last light
from her mother's eyes—shreds of sky.
You're not being still enough, she chides
her friend, though she has made no move
to bend and wrap the body like someone
winding blue thread around a spool.

THE WATERS OF MEMORY

Something wrapped by the water,
its shadow moving like loose-rooted reeds.
Grass leans to the wind,
a kind of song.
What lies hidden might be bones,
the whole skeleton or only the skull.
Sometimes the sky is pure blue,
but even then the thick reeds keep the water

the color of mud,
keep what lies wrapped there
closed off, as in a tomb.
Sometimes there are streaks of blue,
quick, like moving veins.

ARCHITECTURAL THREAD

Before books, when the forgotten was forever
lost, Quintilian discovered he could link
ideas to objects in the rooms of a building,
then walk through the rooms in his mind,
recalling the ideas in order. Centuries later,
Peter of Ravenna decided a deserted church
would better serve. The world meant grief,
but empty stalls might open to devotion
or atonement. If, during one's meditation,
a bird happened to fly through the torn roof
and flutter to rest in the choir,
all movement in the mind should cease
until the bird disappeared into sky.
In this way memory would know
how it felt to lose touch with itself yet keep
going like the thread of the infinite,
blue, or shifting to blue.

ORDINARY BLUE SEA

When Prince Henry the Navigator
sent his mariners from Portugal into
the watery unknown,
each one spinning out from him like a thread
into the Sea of Darkness,
the first of them were afraid to sail their caravels
past Cape Bojador, where red sand

ran like blood from the cliffs
and the sea boiled at the shore.
Then, in 1434, Gil Eannes sailed through
the shadow of fear into the Sea of Darkness.
It was blue, ordinary sea blue.

"BAVARIAN GENTIANS"

The first time she heard the poem
she thought they were actual torches.
She had never heard the word *gentians*.
After that she carried the torches with her
wherever she went. Fringed gentians
and closed gentians. She chose only blue.
The root of the yellow was too bitter,
like sunlight on the day a loved one dies.

TONGUED BELLS

Linnaeus had to speak of the stamen and pistil
in ways that would not offend.
He could not say *sexual organs*.
So instead he described
the *bridegroom* and the *bride*.
The *bridal bed*.
He himself was unable to look at a woman
without thinking of flowers.
The moist parts.
The faint blue veins.
When he named them, putting
the species name along with the genus,
he said it was like
putting the clapper with the bell.

TRANSUBSTANTIALITY

One morning the delphinium,
still belled with night, shook her
as wind might shake her,
down to the root.
So slight!
If the spirit survived the body,
it would be like the blue of this
flower passing to sky,
its roots adrift.

BLUE THREAD

Whole cities lay buried
under earth, and with them
the bodies of royals,
their faces preserved beneath
gold masks. At Mycenae,
when Schliemann dug slowly
to what he thought was
Agamemnon's tomb, the gold lay scattered
like little suns. He took up
the gold death mask from the figure
of the king. There was still a face.
Instantly it began to disintegrate
from the force of air, mere air,
blue thread of time.

THE SLEEP OF BIRDS

Sometimes when she heard
the blue-hued voices of the birds,
she knew that grief came to the body
like a kind of sleep, to give it pause

from the harder occupations of love and faith.
Meanwhile trees held on at the root
and birds went on pressing the air
from their feathers like the vows
a lover might seem to begin
but never finished.

MORNING IN THE SCRIPTORIUM

The monk's robe is stained with broth
and sweat from summer
though now his hands numb with cold.
He has to keep laying the pen beside the fine vellum
to blow on his fingers. There can be no fire
for fear of everything going to ash.
Now he picks up the brush, dips it into the inkpot,
draws the form of a tree. Takes another brush
to apply blue sky, stares down
while it dries. Is he dreaming?
The blue keeps unbolting like silk.
No, like the word of God.
On his lips like a tongue, but no
alphabet for it.

GRASS TONGUES

She knelt in blue-eyed grass.
If she stared long enough at the flowers,
the tiny irises, she could feel herself
shrinking, little bitty hands and feet,
little berry mouth.
Her dress no more than a pocket.
She needed to go inside, not the house
but the body, needed to slip through
one of the passages, pupil or ear,

to see what she kept hiding.
Probably it was many-eyed like the grass.
Not a monster, but many-eyed.
Like the self. Going out every day
and being recognized, called to,
while inside the eyes were whispering
like grass in wind,
codes she could get to if she were resolute,
if she kept from flinching
when the truth spread before her
like the grass, many-eyed,
many-tongued.

PACIFIC DREAM

The water was a blue breast.
There were only three ships left.
They had threaded the maze—

> the narrowest, most devious,
> most circuitous of all the straits
> between two great bodies of water—

managed not to wreck against rocks
as they emerged from the fjord—
eaten biscuit that was nothing

> but powder of biscuit swarming
> with worms—

and now this body of water, blue,
and veined slightly by mild wind—
veined like a breast. A fluke:
for three months and twenty days
over twelve thousand miles, they saw
no storms. So they named it what
you would expect men to name
a breast they learned to dream on.

SKY GENTIANS

Words had colors,
she had known this
since the beginning,
red of cartwheel,
green of sleep,
brown of sick room.
Sorrow was blue,
and death. Blue death
had entered her mother
through the feet,
blue feet cold as sky.

AZURE

Giotto used lapis lazuli for the sky
and sometimes for the robe of the Virgin.
It was an extravagance.
First the grinding and mixing of the stone.
Then the risk of making
a mistake with the quick-drying fresco.
To calm himself he imagined he was painting with sky.
With amplitude.
If doubt came to him, even the least thread,
he broke it off between his teeth.

ARACHNID LEGACY

Weaving is the art of lacing threads together
at right angles. After a while, the fingers
move the threads from memory.

DUST HIEROGLYPHS

She dreamed another Blue Nile,
narrower, more even in its flow
through the veins of mothers
who pleaded to the blue length
to be granted the dispensation
of death before their children
so as not to be left with a wound
nothing would fill, not the moon,
not the sweet nights of the body,
not even the beauty of the world,
which would be as dust to them,
dust, the least vein, dust.

LAST THINGS

Each time she thought of her mother
moving among the dead
she shuddered to remember the passage
where Mme Defarge, asked what
she is knitting, answers *Shrouds*.
She made her mother's shroud of blue thread.
That way, though the blue might fade,
it would still resemble sky or water,
be part of the world
that goes on without us.

THE CORDONING

The houses of the famous dead
are exhausted.
They long to become bone,
lie down like skeletons and be done

while the broken comb on the dresser,
the dented pot and spoon,
the opaque mirrors
float into oblivion—

anything to escape the tedium
of footstep and murmur
beyond the roped-off section
year after year: *So-and-so slept here.*

If you die before I do,
I'll be those multitudes,
come to mourn you.
Standing amazed that the bed

betrays no sign of loss—
the hand-stitched quilt,
worn linens,
the line I'll long to cross.

WINTER FLOWERS

She set the bulbs to root in glass vases
on the windowsill. Narcissi, amaryllis.
Within days, the pale green tusks
of root would start. By the time
the field was deep with snow,
they'd be in bloom. She had to keep

life going. The doctors said she might
not outlive Spring. It was the worst kind
of cancer. Every morning she recited
the list of things she'd never do
until the words seemed common
as the names of common flowers.

She'd stand sipping tea, staring
into the bulbs: *House in Ireland.*
Child. Book. One morning
she noticed the papery lids
had peeled back until the bulbs
seemed eyes—the backs of eyes,

rooting down with the codes
things are given to live by.
She stirred them in the water.
Let it be a blind going like that.
Let the last breaths drift to the surface
calm as longrooted flowers.

BED AND BONE

I can't wait to sleep in my own bed
I kept saying, sometimes to no one,
sometimes as provocation

to be left alone, so by the time
I came home and unpacked, I half
expected the bed to rise in greeting

like a lover, but it just lay there, dumb,
flat, I saw it wouldn't take off
so much as a sock if it were a man,

I would have to do everything,
but I went to it anyway, smiling,
beyond shame, I lay down and sighed

to my bed, that shifted a little as if afraid
I might weep, as I sometimes did,
but not now, now I was about to sleep

in my bed when suddenly I saw
how it would look like other beds
stripped of its covers, as I would look

without my hair and flesh—
and it was then, dear friend,
that grief took hold and shook me

back to that summer in Ithaca,
when, tired of *Ulysses*, we'd walk
from the dorm to stand below the waterfall,

dazed by how quick all passage is.
Bed to bone to nothing.
Mine, then gone.

BOUNDLESS KINGDOM

In the dream my father did the forbidden
so I would know the difference between
"the prince of light and dark"
What darkness would allow such betrayal
of a father twelve years dead

What darkness would allow me to wonder
if the dream were memory speaking
when I know he'd have given his life for me
Did give his life for me, forsaking art
to buy me coats, shoes, bread

The bed in the dream was narrow as a vein

I awoke to my own cries and no one
there to soothe me as my father would
if he could come back from the dead
though he would need to gather his ashes
from the sea where we poured them

and fuse to one of those fish
that seem fluid glass, mere streaks for bones
moving toward me as I stood at the shore
to call and call my sorrow at betrayal
He would hear me and leap for the air

shattering the surface as if it too were glass

I would wade in, bend toward him, my long hair
dark with water, my hands empty of all but the weight
of water moving with the constancy of blood
through my wrists up my arms to the heart contracting
with the effort of keeping track of him

as he slipped deeper off, untouchable as light

THE DEAD STOP, THEY JUST STOP

When he died, I dreamed nothing for months.
Or nothing that I remembered. But I'd wake

to feel my spine sinking deeper into the bed.
To lull my own fears, I *said* I dreamed,

sometimes of him in the leather chair, reading books
backwards, as if to trick his way back into life.

But I'd know to thumb his eyelids shut, take the book,
utterly practical and not the least unhinged . . .

Of course I dreamed, everyone does, but why had I
become one of those who couldn't remember?

His death was not sudden. The usual decline:
bone and loose skin, glazed eyes. For days his spirit

tried to come back, but there was no room left
in the diminishment: this, after a life spent insisting

the dead stopped, they just stopped—. I wanted
to follow, wailing *Daddy!* like the child I was.

In the dreams, that is. I remember them now.
I understand the heaviness in my spine

came from knowing I would wake a grown woman
weeping after her father as she had wept after lovers.

Don't get me wrong. I never lay in my father's arms
except as a child, purely tended. That's why I long

to go back. Then, when he died again, I would know
to mourn with all of my body. I would not try to stop.

43

RED CAMELLIAS SMASHED BY WEEK-LONG RAIN

One night I carried the knives from the house
and buried them under a rock at the back.
After the knives, the razors and ropes. I knew
if he woke he would harm me. But he slept
his drunken sleep on the couch while I went
skillfully past. In the morning he would wake first,
cold, disgruntled, all that evil sour in his mouth.
I would feign sleep above him while he heated
water, banged his cup. Later, when he cried
for his razor, I would slip under the covers.
How could I, a child, have known that dread
was making way for something worse,
remorse that would bite me year after year
because I mistook as violence his deep despair.

CEREMENT

Maybe by now you are near a shore
where you can see her, the deep blue silk
spilled across her knees, her dark head
bowed to the gold thread
of her embroidery. She is making
a robe for her father, a longevity robe
for him to wear on his birthday
when he will pray to the gods to keep him
and his devoted daughter.

Not what you did on that birthday
I gave you a handful of poems,
five long needles I slid at your heart.
I've never been much for poetry
you said on the phone weeks later.
Then nothing but that near silence
I always heard as the sea, caught somewhere
in the lines between us.

If you could see close up, you would notice
her fingers are callused,
so although the needle pricks them,
there's no blood on the silk.
Your ashes disappeared
in the sea where we poured you. Still,
I long to give you a robe.
Not the robe of water you already have,
with its gold of kelp.
No, rich silk that would slip like breath around you.

THEIR BODIES LAY SO FAR

Each night the self lay down to escape
gravity. Even those in the highest beds
felt themselves curve
to the world's surface and begin
the slow spin like an infant,
fist bunching the blanket,
eyes shut.

Then the veer into space.
Some took horses. Some ran.
Some flew as if the sharp bones
had been wings all along.
All around them the dark, the cold fires.
How it tired them, the keeping going,
while their bodies lay so far away.

When it was almost day, rush
of shoe and spoon, the self
that had gone all that time
into nothing
slipped back into the brain
like a shadow of the moon's other side.
Or the death shadow,

close as the skin.
Over time the self would try
to rid itself of this but wake many-skinned
like a snake unable to molt.
And the self would know the heaviness
of lightest moments,
keeping going with its dead.

THREE

THE MAP OF BETRAYAL

Oh farther than everywhere! Oh farther than everywhere!

Pablo Neruda

SUPPER

How does a mother do it,
give you her terrors like
food, *Here, take and eat,*

so you eat, you grow strong
though you lie awake nights
weak in your bones,

you know how fast the door
would break down if
someone tried to get in,

so you study locks, evasions,
you map out escape routes
in dreams, and all this time

your mother is saying *Don't tell
your name if they can hurt you*
not in words but in milk, meat,

she lays everything on a plate
and you eat, eat, you are bone
of her bone, will be dust of her dust,

you go on with the meal she has
set you while you dream of escape
routes, of saying your name

to a man who takes your heart
in his hands like food he can't live
without, until you say *Did you know*

you were eating my mother then wait
to see what he does, if he swallows,
if you can breathe on your own.

RITUALS

Summer, the loft on Spring Street
where I lived with the first one,
where I would stand at the window
every night, smoking,
watching a woman in a studio
across the street, one floor down.
She painted with a frenzy of strokes,
often standing nude before the canvas
so that when the man entered
no time would be wasted
in his entering her.
I would light another cigarette then,
watching with detachment as if I were
watching dogs coupling, the word
my mother had used to explain
what our dog was doing on the lawn
with the neighbor's dog, the frenzied
thrusting. As soon as they stopped
the woman would get up, put on a shirt,
a man's shirt, shiver into it.
Sometimes the man would return
with a cup of something warm
and the woman would take it
with both hands and sip, then
reach to brush his hair back
from his brow. This tenderness
my signal to turn from
the window, weak with longing.
Some nights he stood
beside me, the two of us
smoking, watching,
our own frenzy afterward
the first phase of our uncoupling.

THE YEAR BEFORE THE BREAKUP

I never wanted to go.
I wanted to stay in bed with my blankets
and quilt, my books and lamp.
I twisted my feet in the top sheet.
I pulled the quilt to my chin.

When my mother came in I lay unblinking.
I know you're awake.
Why couldn't she leave me alone?
I could read all day, using up nothing
but my bit of oxygen, light.

Why did I have to sort the darknesses out
the way I would one day sort out
my lover's socks? Matching dark to dark,
thinking of his ankle bone so near,
whispering *Don't ever leave me.*

Not a plea. A threat I could barely
follow. If I'd gone earlier to the forest,
would it have been different?
Would I know why I'm so awake
each time I hear the word?

Forest. Forest.
I know it's in me. I'm just not sure how long
I can carry it, what I'll say the next time
my lover takes me by the shoulders:
What's wrong? You seem

so distant.
How I'll tell him I feel shadows
unpack from the back
of my neck like the trackless cries
I can't stop making.

IF THE NAMES OF THINGS COULD BE RELIED ON

In the Giotto fresco, all eyes
look toward the dying saint
but those of the young friar, who gazes
toward the divine.

If we follow all the lines
between the eyes and the object
of their vision, we see that they're implied lines: there,
though not exactly visible.

How often we let things go
unnoticed in ordinary life—forgetting
to look for signs we know exist. *Who's this* **we?**
he took to saying

toward the end whenever I tried
to implicate myself in his desires.
Then he would look past me—his line of vision implying
a falling away

enough to terrify anyone who clung
to ordinary life—and the snowbirds
that should have been white if the names of things
could be relied on

would lift from the oaks while I sat
waiting for something definite to be said
or done. The surprise came not in his leaving or mine—
mine, as it happened—

but in the way, when I looked back on it,
I could see all the implied lines
between us, so visible they might have been veins.
They emptied like veins.

BLOODSTREAMS

This morning, running stairs in the cul-de-sac
shaded by oak and wild plum, I had to will myself on
Rush of breath and blood
until the world seemed less than there

So I don't know how long the deer had stood
antlered and still in the road
They come down from the hills
in dry season, stopping for fruit leaves and roses

They stare back

I thought of you then, on the other edge
of the country, restless for hunting, the guns and bright vest
brought down from the attic, the cold nights of lying awake,
dreaming of deer falling or not falling, like the long-ago first one,
dragging you on with its splashed blood, your voice a thin-
          bladed whine
you would have sworn was not your own

Finally it was there in a hollow,
stiffening on dark wet leaves
You were afraid there would be no antlers
You knelt, eyes half-closed, and put out your hand
for the warm horn, the sparse surprising hair

No woman would get to you like that, you told me

I stayed awake night after night
planning an escape you couldn't follow
I thought it would be that simple,
the door would close behind me
like a season

I didn't know you'd kneel and touch my hair,
the closest you could come to pleading
as my body closed against you

I didn't know what you did,
how the blood between us could go
anywhere, and would

PENITENT

I used to sit watching him thinking
it was wrong to have married him
because I loved him the way I loved
what was wounded. I'd think back to
birds I'd watch as a kid, flying headlong
into our plate-glass windows, snapping

their necks, so many dead that pretty soon
I'd just scoop them up and toss them
down the bank. No more spoon-dug graves
or twig crosses, and if they weren't dead,
if I saw them twitching on the shale,
I'd go on with my game or climb higher

into the maple, skinning the heels of my palms
though I wouldn't have called this penitence,
as the nights I lay awake beside his snores
weren't penitence, just refusal to do what I had to.
It took so long. I kept walking away from it
the way I did those birds, until the day

I found the bones of one intact, the
feathers still on it, so phantom, a bone
bird, and when I tried to slide it onto a leaf
it came apart like air. Afterwards I thought
I must have imagined it. I was always seeing
God in moss or standing water, his long cloak

swept to his neck in a rush of rebuke.
You spend too much time dreaming
my mother would say, but when I finally
said it, said what I had to, I got through it
by imagining my words as birds,
flying into the invisible

wall between us.
Crows or starlings. Black, a greasy sheen.
Nothing pretty about it. Nothing penitent
in the way I said I was sorry,
said it over and over,
my words coming apart like air.

ARCHER

I never meant to hurt you
the lover swears at the end.
You know the scene: someone
standing, hand toward the door
while the world goes on as if nothing
has changed. For a time, the one
left behind makes no move.
As if an arrow had entered the heart.

Then rage, mess, insult of memory:
I never meant . . .
Until one night the words fly out of the moon,
out of sleeves in the closet.
All of them sharp-tipped.
All of them hissing.
All of them entering the heart repeatedly.
And there is no death.

And this is what was meant.

BORDER WARS

ENDLESS JUNCTURE

One night I woke borderless.
I writhed and turned,
hoping to wrap the white sheet
into form, into body.
But there was only stillness
of the less-than-there:
vapor trail, unplayed air.

METEMPSYCHOSIS

In thick sacks in the hospital lab
the amputated limbs lay stacked.
*Would you care to save the limb
for burial?* the amputees were asked.
I stood by while my grandmother
said her dancing days were over.
The doctor stared at arms and legs
cut off, dancing into dust.

TRANSMOGRIFIED PAIN

To prove that my heart
did not ache, was impervious
to whatever pain he might try
to inflict, I unbuttoned my dress,
opened my breast, lifted out
my heart and held it in the flame
of the candle between us.
You're bloodless he murmured.
I slid the heart back,

stitched the skin back up
finely as linen and spat: bad luck
to sew upon oneself. The candle
and his wonder hissed.

THE GODDESS OF CARPE DIEM

People die in their beds,
in water or air, under ground,
in the street. So why not covet joy:
full-bodied fruit, full-bodied light
touching the least-bodied insect or plant
cavorting with the wind, never thinking
Something is going to happen
or *This is bound to end.*

ARCHAIC REMNANTS

My mother kept the compact
high on the bathroom shelf,
its mirror cloudy with time and powder.
I crept in to open it, watch
the apple trees at the window
tilt and vanish, reappear.
My own face came to me in pieces.

THE FRAGMENT

The snake coiled, tail in mouth,
on the warm stone.
I was not frightened.
I felt pity, a need to cry out.
My mouth was not my own.

I keep all the keys in a tin.
One by one they enter me:
the room where my mother wept,
the attic where spiders fattened,
the cellar where my father slept,
bed where I keep opening.
I pass through borders at will.
And when people ask *Who are you?*
I open the tin,
I let them choose.

THE MUSE OF THE ACTUAL

She'd hate if her mother were proved right—
that having her, he'd never leave his wife.
We were sitting on the back deck, looking
at the apple trees, that had fluttered white
a week ago, but now were green and plain.

We blew our black tea cool while she told me
the other day he'd sat where I was sitting,
to paint the hill, the trees, and, so she would
think of him each time she looked, a bull,
pawing a fallen apple in the foreground.

I guess you could call it a self-portrait,
she laughed, and went laughing to get it
from her bedroom, then propped it against
the deck rail in the shade of the grape trellis
so we could sit looking back and forth

from the painted hill to the actual,
identical except for the bull, who did
resemble him, hunched forward, restless.
He does that, she said after a while.
Sort of paws around. I mean with me.

She swirled her tea and sipped.
Sometimes it's like he's still painting.
Smudging things. His tongue
working away like a brush—his tongue
and other things. I keep thinking

I should ask if he sees me as fallen.
A sigh. *The truth is I like being*
the muse. He hadn't painted for years.
Now love had restored his desire.
Her own desire was never so intense

as in the moment he drove off again,
back to the wife in Ithaca. *Talk about
myth*, she said. I stared at the bull,
half expecting it to turn into him,
burst from the canvas, wild with love

for her and willing to forsake the world
to prove it. But I knew the world
was closer to her mother's version.
Whatever the miracles of art, the bull
would stay put, like the laws of the actual.

THE DOUBLE

She was chopping cilantro when she told me,
the green going black with the force of the blade.
I've been killing myself in my dreams ever since.
Sometimes I don't remember.
But when I wake and the room
looks like a package with the wrong address
I know I've done it again.
Often it was death by drowning.
But there were plane crashes, poison.

Thwack! By now the cilantro lay withered
at the edge of the cutting board,
and she was working an onion into a pile
of little teeth. Milk teeth or seed teeth;
I looked away. When I turned back,
I could see her bones. She was slicing peppers
into thin red tongues and at first I saw only
her arm bones, quick knuckles.
Then the rib cage, the flat spoons of her knees.
Her spine was a milky rope.
I couldn't tell what held the skull so still.

It was then I noticed the dreams.
They were stored like discs, with pictures
as labels. Her holding a dog by the throat.
Her opening a plane door in midair.
Her ladling soup with bare hands from a black tureen.

All this time she was going on with the salad.
She had salad every night, she said, with bread and wine.
There was that life, and the life in the skull.
The one body, that he had said didn't interest him
anymore. Not brutally—there was grief
in his voice. *As if I had already died* she said.
As if he were telling me the awful news.

TALKING ABOUT THE WEATHER

While the hurricane stalls off the coast
and coastal waters surge with it,
while persistent drought in the heartland
stunts the corn and turns the earth to dust,
I stack wood against winter, saying
Summer's just not long enough
because already the nights are cool,
any day now I'll drive into town and
notice the poplars at Ramos's farm
have begun to turn, and I'll begin
longing for winter's terrible drama.
Snow squalls so wild last December
even the wide-winged plows shut down . . .

Or so I imagined when I saw on CNN
that intermittent lake-effect snow would persist
all over the eastern end of Lake Ontario.
I was here, the other side of the country,
where fire or mudslides threaten half the year,
earthquakes every minute. *The Big One*
could come as you are reading this
the paper says. I still haven't bought
a preparedness kit, though I know
what to do about the gasline, where
the extra water is, the good flashlight,
extra batteries. There's enough tinned food
to last two families a month . . .

                                    I tell you this
as if it's news, as if it's my house not yours
we live in, because the other conversation,
the one I'm carrying on anyway under all
this talk of weather and catastrophe,
is so much harder over the same dinner

we've had a dozen times this month, and the month
before it. The one where I tell you I can feel
a bad storm coming, wanting you
to point to a sunstrewn sky and say
What are you talking about, it's beautiful.
And everything reverses: I'm the one
who's talking about the weather.

THE SPHERE OF CÉZANNE'S APPLES

It was one of those days when birds go quiet and trees
refuse to be anything but trees. I was reading
about Cézanne, wondering what it would be like to have
my portrait painted by someone intent on rendering contrasts.
Probably I would not look as sad as his wife Hortense,

but my skin would look worn, my eyes would sink back
with the weight of failures, which Cézanne would see
as clearly as he saw the sphere of the apple, the cones
of hill and mountain. Thinking this was sentimental,
I knew, and then I couldn't stop thinking of you,

how what I love about Cézanne's apples is what I love
about you: You don't pretend to be what you aren't.
You won't claim more than you feel, even when I plunge
past shame or scruple to ask *Do you love me?*
Sometimes this makes me feel like poor Hortense,

faithful, long-serving but unsung. But then I remember
the portrait Cézanne did of her with her hair unpinned.
Her head tilts insecurely, but you can tell how solid
he believed her. A face still as an apple. The ribbons
on her dress curve for her breasts, form yielding

to form. Like your hand at my thigh. How everything
shifts then to allow its opposite, love and doubt like apples
we eat for sweetness or leave in the blue bowl
until we toss them under the coast oaks for birds
who might carry the seed for miles, like song.

THE MAP OF BETRAYAL

We were in bed, talking about betrayal,
naming different kinds of it like minerals
or kingdoms, slowing down once we had
a dozen or so, as if we were coming to
the ones we ourselves were guilty of,

or that's what I was thinking, so mostly
to distract myself, I said, *And death,*
death's probably the biggest one of all.
But he, with lawyer's logic, said definitely
not: If everyone knew from the get-go

that death would come, then how could
death betray? No, death was part
of the code, whereas betrayal involved
breaking it, slipping it to the enemy—
some violation or trespass that the blood

would know forbidden—not mindless obedience
to a bound-to-be end. *Listen,* I told him,
if you died tomorrow, I'd feel betrayed.
It'd be like losing you to a thousand women.
He stared past me while the night sky

filled with stars, a half moon. *The stars*
are dying, he said. *And we're the stuff*
of stars. So if death were betrayal,
that would make the sky betrayal's map.
He often deflected things this way,

by way of conceding impasse.
It was reason enough to dread
losing him, I thought, turning out
the lights to study the map better.
In another millennium, people would

be buying package tours to Orion,
the Pleiades, living in space colonies.
Making room for more betrayals,
which would still come one by one.
Like death, I whispered while he slept.

I DON'T WANT ALL OF YOU

Just past the exit to the canyon road
the hills dip to a hollow
thick with trees that lure me
with their shadows, their stillness.
Even in wind they seem still.
The leaves go black as I look,
though I look quickly,
part of me headed north to work,
the rest longing to move among the trees
as a deer would, stopping
for leaf or root, some signal
my ears could flick from the wind.
It's not that I'm lost or directionless.
It's not that I want a new life.
I just want the stillness
trees know, or deer take on
when they move among the trees,
obeying the natural order.
I want to lift my head to the wind
and dip it down again,
tree, deer, lover,
taking no more
than what's needed.

FIELD GUIDE

We were walking through bear grass,
partridgefoot, picking out avalanche
lilies, white bog orchids as if they were
familiars in our dreams, the landscape
neurons had constructed for the times

when the body keeps back like a shy
or lazy child and the spirit is forced to go
naked, bear what is to be borne, fire, ruin,
we even saw a wild rose called firethorn,
spreading out from the foundations

of lost buildings, which we carried as frames
for our stories, knowing we would need a sense
of place, not wanting to lose each other
to the drift of mind through what can never
be wholly told since it goes on faster

than clouds carrying the weather across
nights of love and talk, across the lights
of fieldless cities or below the moon and stars
in rural dark, where so little of time's ruin
can be seen, though suddenly a spread of

pearly everlasting on the path reminded us
that even if houses sank on their foundations
or lovers kept whispering in embrace while
stream orchids bloomed and died and bloomed
and insects climbed the bleeding heart

or Jacob's ladder, we would need to stay
many-eyed like the grass as we moved back
to the real, to a room where our senses would
fill with each other's bodies as they might
with fireweed, shooting star, tall violet and bell.

ABOUT THE AUTHOR

Lynne Knight was born in Philadelphia, Pennsylvania, and grew up in Cornwall-on-Hudson, New York. She graduated from the University of Michigan and from Syracuse University, where she was a fellow in poetry. After living for a time in Canada, she returned to the States with her daughter and taught high school English in upstate New York before moving to California in 1990. Her first collection, *Dissolving Borders*, won a *Quarterly Review of Literature* prize in 1996 and was published as part of its Contemporary Poets Series. A cycle of poems on Impressionist winter paintings, *Snow Effects*, appeared from Small Poetry Press as part of its Select Poets Series (2000). Her second full-length collection, *The Book of Common Betrayals*, won the Dorothy Brunsman Award from Bear Star Press in 2002. Her work has appeared in a number of journals, including *Kenyon Review, New England Review, Ontario Review, Poetry, Poetry Northwest* and *Southern Review*. One of her poems appears in *Best American Poetry 2000*, selected by Rita Dove. Among her other awards are the Theodore Roethke Award from *Poetry Northwest*, the Theodore Christian Hoepfner Award from *Southern Humanities Review*, and the Rosalie Moore Special Award from *Blue Unicorn*. She lives in Berkeley and teaches writing part-time at two Bay Area community colleges.

DATE DUE

GAYLORD			PRINTED IN U.S.A.